To Elana.

The Universe is constantly sending us messages — listen!

Reflections ♡
From Beyond

Sharing a Message of Hope,
Peace and Kindness

While it is traditional for the author to compose the dedication, Tracy La Croix, the man whose journey is being shared in this book, has requested the opportunity to do so. Thus, with my wholehearted agreement, I am honoring his request:

Tracy dedicates this book to his wife, Alice, for everything that she has gone through and for her continued support and care.

And to CJ's friends and neighbors in Newtown, CT as she and they continue to heal from the unthinkable tragedy that took place at the Sandy Hook Elementary School on December 14, 2012.

Also by CJ Golden

Tao of the Defiant Woman
*Five Brazen Ways to Accept What You Must
and Rebel Against the Rest*

Tao-Girls Rule!
*finding balance, staying confident, being bold
in a world of challenges*

FOREWORD

Coincidence? Serendipity? Do they exist? This powerful book will make you reflect upon these concepts when thinking about the limitations of "existing."

For forty plus years I have studied and worked with patients near death - as a critical care nurse and as a hospice nurse. I have learned that these patients are not just tragic victims of life-threatening situations, but rather enlightened beings yearning to teach us the truths they have experienced that will enrich our living and our dying, will bring us peace in grieving and remove our fear of what, if anything, lays ahead.

And imagine the "coincidence" of a gifted writer from a town heartbroken with grief, meeting, in the most unlikely of places, an enlightened being with a powerful message of healing with hope, peace and kindness that needed telling.

"To know the road ahead, ask those returning." Chinese proverb

Maggie Callanan

Maggie Callanan, RN, author of *Final Journeys* and co-author of *Final Gifts*, is the coordinator of the National

Hospice, Palliative and Home Care Speakers Bureau, and has served as a board member of the International Association of Near-Death Studies (IANDS) and the facilitator of the IANDS National Capitol Area Chapter support group for near-death experiencers.

Ms. Callanan is a world-renowned speaker on topics relating to the care of the dying, as well as coping strategies for hospice staff and volunteers.

Prologue:

June 5, 2012

"I was on the hospital bed
when my heart stopped beating.
And I found myself on a white path
heading towards a bright light."

Tracy LaCroix
Cape Charles, VA

May 3, 2013

"Driving the support vehicle for Joe and his buddies,
we stopped at a charming little hotel in Cape Charles,
Virginia.
Why here? Why now?
And then I met Tracy LaCroix."

CJ Golden
Newtown, CT

> *"The universe is always speaking to us...sending us little messages,*
> *causing coincidences and serendipities, reminding us to stop, to*
> *look around, to believe in something else, something more."*
> *~Nancy Thayer*

PART ONE

A Meeting of Two Souls

"It's a bizarre but wonderful feeling, to arrive dead center of a target you didn't even know you were aiming for."
~Lois McMaster Bujold

Chapter One

CJ: The Prophetic Encounter

I am a woman who has learned to follow her path and understand that it will take me where it will, even if the direction appears to be rather off-course. I suspect that happens to many of us - if not all - for there we are, going along quite contentedly when a roadblock appears or a detour sign pops up in front of us. "This is not what I expected, nor what I planned," we moan. "What shall I do now with this new set of circumstances?"

Well, what I do, is recognize that it is what it is, I am where I am, the world around me is rotating as it is supposed to and it is up to me to find the meaning behind this new development in my life. While the cosmos might have handed me an unexpected complication, while I might have been guided to make a left turn rather than the right turn in my life's GPS as anticipated, it is completely my choice to do with that turn what is best for me and for those whom I love.

It was such a circumstance that took me to a charming little hotel in Cape Charles, Virginia, where I met Tracy

LaCroix and learned of his dramatic "heart-stopping" journey.

Observing me pull into the parking lot of the hotel that would serve as my home away from home that auspicious day - May 3, 2012 - manager Tracy LaCroix hopped off his tractor and walked through the manicured field he had been mowing. Greeting me with a warm and welcoming smile, he cheerfully completed the registration paperwork and handed me my room key. And we briefly chatted about how we both came to be in this lovely little town.

While registering new guests is usually his wife, Alice's, job, she happened to have been off-property for a short span of time - a span of time that allowed this serendipitous meeting between a man with a dramatic journey to share and a writer who was open, and eager, to bring his words and message to the world.

And so began the saga that led to the writing of this book. Both Tracy and I have endeavored to not highlight any one specific religious aspect of life - for that is too individual a realm for us to venture into - but to emphasize the spiritual side of our lives that we all too often tend to disregard.

Spirituality, in my humble opinion, differs from religion in that it does not require a specific deity. Spirituality is that which helps us follow our paths, brings us to certain crossroads, leads us down one road or another and, in doing so, teaches us the lessons we need to learn so our lives have meaning.

If you do not yet believe that there is an ultimate force in the Universe helping to guide us, then hopefully, after reading of Tracy's journey you will begin to open your eyes, hearts and souls to the infinite potentials that lie outside of our understanding.

I was not necessarily a very spiritual person when I began this project, although I was open to any and all possibilities. For who am I to disbelieve merely because science has not yet found analytical proof?

And because of the serendipity of my meeting Tracy and learning of his journey, life has become more meaning-ful and its ebbs and flows exquisitely complete.

I believe, without any doubt, that I had been chosen by forces I may never understand to bring Tracy's story to the world; to help Tracy share his message of hope, peace and kindness, with all who meet him – whether through this book or hearing his words in person.

According to Tracy, when we first met there was some-thing about me that let him know I was a woman who needed to share his journey. He understood why when

I told him that I live in Newtown, Connecticut. His first words to me were "That's why you are here." He continued by imploring me to bring back his message of healing and peace, to my friends and neighbors. And, so, to the people of Newtown, Tracy and I sincerely hope his words find a place in your hearts and souls and bring some comfort.

Chapter Two

CJ: Guided To Tracy

It was in May of 2013 when my husband, Joe, and his two cycling buddies were enjoying a weeklong journey through Delaware, Maryland and Virginia down the Delmarva Peninsula. Not a cyclist, but not wanting to miss out on the adventure, I was driving the route in our bright little red car with the large bicycle rack on the back. Purportedly, I was the support wagon, local scout and cheering squad, but mostly I was me, writer and inveterate nosy-body, stopping along the trail to talk to the "locals."

I did, indeed, meet many folks along the way; each who had his or her own story to share, but it is Tracy LaCroix who stands out among the rest. It is Tracy and his remarkable journey that changed the way I look at life and opened up my soul to the magical possibilities the Universe has to offer.

Joe, his pals and I had left our hotel in Exmore, Virginia, on the morning of May 3rd and traveled a mere twenty-two miles to our destination in Cape Charles. On each of the previous cycling days the guys rode an average of fifty or sixty miles. Why, then, we wondered, did we lay out the route to include a stop in this little town? Our next day's destination, Virginia Beach, Virginia, was only forty-three miles away and could surely have been reached directly from Exmore without this "unnecessary" stop. We also questioned the reasoning behind choosing to spend the night at this particular hotel, which is situated on the main highway rather than right in town. There was a hotel in the heart of Cape Charles itself, yet here we were – six miles away.

But upon presenting ourselves at the front desk, Joe and I met innkeeper Tracy LaCroix. Enjoying his warm welcome, we recognized that this had been a very fine choice of hotels for it was, indeed, charming - comfortable and comforting, the rooms large, bright and airy. We were quite content.

Tracy is a strapping fifty-one-year-old man who had to leave his tractor and unfinished lawn work to take our check-in information and hand us the key to our room. His is a big presence, both in physical size and charm. With a soft-spoken manner and easy smile, Tracy is someone with whom one feels immediately relaxed. And so we chatted. In our conversations we spoke mostly of that which brought us here to Cape Charles. Tracy and his wife, Alice, had only arrived and taken up their positions as innkeepers six weeks earlier. Newbies to the area, he and Alice were busy settling themselves into their new environment, meeting the locals and enhancing the hotel with fresh plantings and their personal congeniality.

Chatting with Tracy revealed that he had come down to this part of the country first from New Hampshire, then from Springfield, Massachusetts.

Discrete prodding on my end, coupled with an eagerness to talk on Tracy's part, allowed me to discover that his was a not-so-unusual story of the ultra successful, world-traveling salesman who found himself laid-off during the recession several years ago. But, not ones to sit back and bemoan the situation, Tracy and Alice immediately began a search for new employment and within two months were both hired as managers for a large retirement community in Springfield, Massachusetts.

Springfield, Massachusetts, is the home of Baystate Medical Center.

Baystate Medical Center is where Tracy had died eleven months *before* I met him.

Chapter Three

Tracy AS TOLD TO CJ: The Invincible Teen

When I met CJ I knew there was a connection but didn't understand it until we began to talk and she interviewed me. I opened up to her and, when she asked if I wanted to write a book, I told her I would do so, if I were a writer.

I didn't realize it, but I had been waiting for the right person to come along; someone who would listen, who would "get it", who would share my journey and my message.

That person was CJ.

And here is my history as I told it to her. Each recalled, physical episode in my life had not made much of an impact on me psychologically, yet with further reflection I now recognize that someone, something, was subtly guiding me. I just didn't understand it at the time.

Born in Bellingham, Washington, I grew up as a military brat who moved many times with my family as my father was relocated from one base to another. We found ourselves in Italy, Maine, Hawaii and DC until my father finally retired to Assonet, Massachusetts, after twenty-three years of service. I was seventeen when we settled in the little town that sat along the river that bore the same name. It was there that I graduated from high school and, not unlike many recent graduates, decided to seek my life's work somewhere else - anywhere else - just as long as I was far away from Assonet and my family.

Hitchhiking around the country with a mere $187.00 in my pocket, I travelled from coast to coast, picking up stray jobs along the way until I ended up back in Washington State. I found employment in the plywood mill where my father, and grandfather before him, had both worked. It was good steady work until four hundred pounds of plywood dropped on my thumb. At the age of nineteen I had to undergo surgery to repair a torn tendon.

Young and strong, my thumb healed quickly and I moved on once more. This time to California and then eventually back to Massachusetts where I stayed with my family for about a month before moving to Loxahatchee, Florida, to do construction work. I was a kid and enjoying my nomadic life.

As much as I liked living at a campground in Loxahatchee, wanderlust took hold again and once more I headed back to Assonet and my folks, and got a job in a spool mill. It didn't take long for my path to change once more, yet this time it was not of my own accord.

A month into my new life at the spool mill, I was a passenger in a car that was involved in an accident - an accident that by all accounts I should not have survived. Yet survive I did. We had been on a desolate stretch of country road when we came around a curve and slid on some wet leaves. The driver, overcorrecting for the skid, sent us, and the car, head-on into a tree. The fortunate part was that we were now in front of the very few houses along that route. With a broken left femur, dislocated right hip and breaks in both ankles there was no way I could exit the car on my own. But, because of those few homes nearby, some people saw what was happening, raced to the scene and pulled me to safety. Just as they set me down on the ground the car exploded in flames.

I do remember sitting there, looking at my leg and wondering how it would get fixed. I did not reflect upon my good fortune of having been rescued "just in the nick of time" nor the reason for my being saved. I was twenty-years-old, a hotshot and invincible.

I awoke in a hospital bed, left leg in traction and heavily sedated. The doctors gave me some options: they could put me in a body cast for six months, or leave me in traction for that same stretch of time, or insert a steel rod from knee to hip and I'd be out of the hospital in six weeks. It was a no-brainer for me. I opted for the rod.

Truth be told, I had a very fine time for myself in that hospital. The staff often came in bringing food, sitting and chatting. Some even brought their daughters along to meet me. And, there was my physical therapist, who taught me to walk again. She came after hours to visit. And a relationship began to grow. So much so that upon my release we had our first dinner date.

Chapter Four

Tracy AS TOLD TO CJ: Finding Myself

Shortly after being released from the hospital, still on crutches, I recall going to a party at a friend's house sometime around New Year's Eve. What I do not remember are the specifics of the altercation in which I had somehow gotten myself involved. I know it had to do with too much liquor and the still-wild spirit within me.

Arriving home, my father, a recovering alcoholic (who was absolutely tyrannically adamant about not drinking) told me I had but a couple of weeks to move out. My behavior was not to be tolerated under his roof.

It was my physical therapist who took me in so I could get back on my feet. Well, that "getting back on my feet" stretched from several months to a year and then two years. And we married.

Working as a shipping receiver at that time, I endured yet another of my unfortunate accidents when the stress of catching fifty pound boxes all day dislocated my shoulder and tore the rotator cuff. More surgery followed. I was becoming aware that I was quite an economic boon to the community of orthopedic surgeons. And it was time to change the behaviors that were bringing me into those situations and were causing me, and those who loved me, physical and emotional pain.

But the kid in me was not yet quite ready to leave and so I bought myself a motorcycle and started riding around with a buddy. One day for some strange reason, I decided I needed to purchase a pair of cycling gloves. I put them on before heading out on a long country road. Suddenly, a parked van decided to pull out next to me. I tried to swerve out of its way but I saw a car approaching. I had no option but to veer away, missing the van by what appeared to be inches. My bike and I headed into the woods, dodging trees, and finally arriving at a clearing near a school. To avoid a playground area I ran into a ditch. I lost control of the handlebars and ended up being forced into the dirt, then bouncing on the asphalt. Sliding on my hands, some of my body got a little road rash, but my new gloves were completely shredded. As happened in the car crash I thought nothing of the accident. I had no concept that I was being watched over or helped by someone or something. Nope. I was still that indestructible kid. Not a big deal.

At the ripe old age of twenty-four I went back to school at the Sylvania Technical School in Waltham, Massachusetts, and specialized in telecommunications and computers. My dream was to work on a space station but that fell apart with the Challenger space shuttle disaster when everyone in the field found themselves being laid-off.

Yet this was the first time I had ever applied myself, found what I was actually made of and discovered there was intelligence within me that I had never allowed to find the light of day. My grade point average, I am proud to say, was ninety-six. I was psyched. And I was ready to finally find my wings and grow up.

My first job out of school was with a company that manufactured spectrometers. I worked with generators, power supplies, and did water and metal analysis. It was a big job and a good one, and I excelled at it.

Fast-forward several years. Forward through my divorce from the therapist. Forward through my rise in the corporate world where I was starting to travel internationally - and did so for ten years. I loved the traveling. I'd land in a country for a month or so, pick up a couple of words in the language, learning how to say, "hello" and "thank you" and "where's the nearest bar."

I even met a young woman who worked for the same company. We were wed and subsequently had two great kids together. I missed much the early years of my first child – my daughter – due to my frequent travelling but when I was home it was a delight to be with her and her brother.

When I left that particular job I went to work for a company that made 3-D laser printers, starting out as a consultant in the service department and eventually becoming the sales engineer for the European market, then for all of Asia and finally for all sales outside of North America.

I was flying high, figuratively and literally. I spent about two months of the year in the air. And I had several close calls. On a plane from Washington Dulles Airport, we had a near miss with a small aircraft flying at the same altitude. Our pilot banked the 727 so hard that we were nearly upside-down. Another flight had me coming into Logan Airport in Boston but we were caught in a fog, found ourselves starting to land in a field rather than the runway, pulled up, circled around and, running low on fuel, finally landed in Newark, New Jersey.

Ah, invincible me. How smugly I just continued to accept that explanation of my numerous misadventures.

And I remained convinced of my invincibility when, living in Manchester, New Hampshire, I was scheduling a flight to Japan. Because the fares were often much higher from Manchester than they were from Logan Airport in Boston, I usually opted to drive the extra distance to Boston and save a bit of money. However, on this particular occasion the fare from Manchester was not much more than from Logan Airport. And, so, on September 11, 2001, I booked the first leg of my flight out of Manchester - not Boston.

It was the Boston to Los Angeles flight that ended up being the first one to crash into the World Trade Center.

Chapter Five

Tracy AS TOLD TO CJ: The Pivotal Breakthrough

Why did I continue to ignore the messages that were being sent my way? The answer is that I just did. My near-fatal car accident, the airplane mishaps, and the motorcycle crash - I just took them all in stride. I never assumed these incidents to be anything more than my invincibility.

Even my close call on September 11, far too fateful to have sloughed off, took on no specific significance for me.

Only now do I realize there had been someone guiding me, keeping me safe and pointing me in a direction that I could not, at that time, recognize. I did know, however, that I was searching for something even though I just didn't know what it was.

By the fall of 2003 I was a recently divorced man - for the travelling had taken a toll on my marriage. This was when I met a young Thai woman who introduced me to Buddhism. I had never accepted my family's Catholic doctrines so I eagerly embraced the spirituality that defines Buddhism, a beautiful and peaceful religion. And this was good. For a while. Living in Manchester, New Hampshire, at the time, I could not find a Buddhist Temple and was not strong enough to practice without the help of others. I continued to feel there was still some great truth missing from my life.

Then I met Alice. Unwinding after work one evening with a hard-earned beer in the local Applebee's Restaurant, I noticed a young woman at the end of the bar sitting with her teen-age daughter. This woman's beauty, while apparent on her features, came from a place deep within her soul. This was a woman who, I knew even from afar, ministered to others through a relationship with God that I wanted to find myself.

Fast-forward through many such silent meetings in that same restaurant until one day Alice walked in, came right over to me and asked about my bike parked outside. It was an innocent question. She wanted to alert me that it might get a drenching when the lawn sprinklers went off. And then she took her place with her daughter, at the end of the bar. But this time, when she left her seat to go to the ladies room, both her daughter and the bartender moved her belongings to the stool next to me.

Our conversation was free and easy. So much so that Alice handed me her card and suggested I give her a call.

Of course I did, and with her daughter's blessings, we had our first date, moved in together within a month, and eventually married.

I continued travelling all over the world during this time in my professional life. That changed, however, when the economy crashed and I was laid off.

It didn't take long for me to find other employment, this time as a groundskeeper at a local golf course. My pay was a drastic cut from that which I was used to but at least it was work and, after I had finished my duties, I could go out and play golf. We made do although it was a tough financial adjustment. My severance pay went very quickly, but with Alice's faith and courage, I flourished emotionally and began to find the belief in God that has kept me strong to this day.

The pivotal moment in my quest to fully embrace the fact that God was now, and always has been, there for me came - in of all places - the county jail.

I had been falsely accused of a crime and ended up in that county jail. The headstrong side of me refused to pay bail and chose to remain behind bars until I could prove my innocence. I was angry. Furious. I asked for a bible, which arrived in my cell three days later. As soon as I touched it I began to cry and all of the guilt that I had carried within melted away.

Strong in the personal resolve that I was not a good person, I had spent all of my life holding on to that unnecessary guilt. It had held me back from realizing my true potential as a caring human being. Grasping that bible let me know I could change my life – with the help of Alice and God – who had, of course, brought her to me.

He had been trying to guide me throughout my life. He had been sending me messages. I just wasn't hearing them. It took Alice and that stint in the county jail to get me to listen.

And listen I did, for during my twenty-eight days of incarceration, I began to minister to the kids who were there with me. When I shared my belief with them, it grew even stronger within me.

Twenty-eight days after the false accusations, I was cleared of all charges and sent back home. And I started attending church and got involved in charitable work. It was a joy.

A year at a foundry as a sales engineer followed. I excelled at that job as I had done in my previous jobs. But when military projects began to dry up I found myself, yet again, unemployed. Not for long, though, because shortly thereafter I saw an ad in an on-line site for a couple who would be willing to manage a large retirement community in Springfield, Massachusetts.

I sent Alice's resume along with mine and within a few short minutes my phone rang. A forty-five minute interview with the recruiting agent for the corporation took place right then and there. Because these folks were going to be in my area in a couple of weeks they requested a face-to-face meeting with both of us.

We passed that four-hour interview with flying colors and were immediately sent to Denver, Colorado, for training. How we loved that city. We hoped we'd be allowed to remain and manage one of the company's properties there but that was not to be. We were told that our jobs would be at one of their communities in Springfield, Massachusetts. I was earmarked for sales and Alice for the day-to-day running of the operation. Tired of sales, however, I decided to hand that position over to Alice and I, in turn, would do the job she had been given.

Not only did that switch work, it worked so well that we were quickly promoted to the top managerial positions. We brought life to the area and became the most successful and well-run community among the thirteen in the region.

We were doing great.

But my body was not.

Chapter Six

Tracy AS TOLD TO CJ: And Then I Died

Alice and I had been at the retirement community almost a year when one day, while moving a couch from the second floor down to the first – with helpers, of course – I heard an ominous pop erupt from my knee. The invincible side of me that still existed to some extent decided to not bother seeking medical attention. The practical side recognized it was time to visit yet another orthopedist.

Because further scrutiny of the affected knee revealed a condition of bone-on-bone, I was given several cortisone shots. They alleviated the pain somewhat, but did not cure the underlying problem. I was slated for total knee replacement surgery.

A pre-op EKG did show some abnormality in my heart but certainly not anything that would inhibit the safe and successful outcome of the surgical procedure. And so, on April 30, 2012 at Baystate Medical Center in Springfield, Massachusetts, I was given a new knee. All was fine and I remained in the hospital to recuperate.

But three days later, just one day prior to my release date, I suffered congestive heart failure. A battery of tests found a blocked artery and also discovered that I had apparently endured a silent heart attack at some point in the past. My heart, trying to correct itself, had done its own bypass but it was working at only seventy-five percent efficiency.

The first plan was to treat me with medications and keep me in the hospital to be monitored. I remained there for three weeks. And then I went home.

And underwent another episode of congestive heart failure.

Back into the hospital I went and stayed another two weeks as the doctors continued to work towards adjusting my medications. But a short week and a half after arriving back home I went into congestive heart failure yet again.

Okay, so back to Baystate where I was given the choice of the insertion of a stent which carried a sixty-five percent probability of success, or bypass surgery which promised a much higher success rate.

After Alice and I (poor Alice, how very emotionally and physically taxing this was on her) and the senior residents at the hospital conferred, it was decided to do the bypass surgery.

On June 4th, 2012 the medical team at Baystate Medical Center performed that surgical procedure on my heart. It was perfect. Textbook perfect. Went off without a hitch. And I was brought to CCU at 7:30 p.m. that evening.

The doctors told Alice I was fine and suggested she go home to get some sleep. In my heavily sedated state, I wouldn't know if she was there even if she stayed to see me. So she wisely followed that advice and left the hospital.

That's when my heart stopped beating.

Chapter Seven

Tracy and Alice
AS TOLD TO CJ:
The Physical Journey

Tracy:

The doctors have no idea why my heart stopped around midnight on June 5th. I was in CCU recuperating from the bypass surgery when the heart monitor I was hooked up to flat-lined.

For an hour and a half two medical teams worked tirelessly to restore my heartbeat during which time they performed CPR and, I am told, used the defibrillator seventeen times. There was a brief period of about ten minutes during the hour and a half when my heart appeared to be beating on its own, but then it stopped just as abruptly as it had done originally. Eventually the doctors opened my chest to manually massage my heart. At 1:20 a.m. the emergency room nurse called Alice to tell her I had passed away. "Please come down," she advised, "and bring a pastor."

I cannot begin to imagine what Alice was going through when that call came. She is an extremely strong woman and somehow held it together as she travelled back to the hospital planning to say her goodbyes to me.

What she had no way of knowing was that the medical teams had – for reasons they themselves cannot explain – kept working on me, and a mere ten minutes after Alice received the nurse's call, my heart started beating on its own. Some time later, when I questioned the team members as to why they kept working on me for so long, their response was that I was young and they felt compelled to keep going.

Alice:
After Tracy's bypass surgery I had been told that he would remain sedated in CCU for a while and there was no reason for me to stay at the hospital. All had gone extremely well, there was no danger and I had much work to accomplish as the manager on-duty for the 147 residents in the retirement community where Tracy and I worked.

It was at 1:20 in the morning when I received the distressing phone call from the emergency room nurse who told me they had lost Tracy. I was to get our pastor and get to Baystate as quickly as possible.

I immediately called my chief of staff who came to the community and took over my responsibilities there so I could go the hospital.

Upon my arrival I was directed to a waiting area where I sat, anxiously, for fifteen hours. I had been told that shortly after I had received the phone call Tracy's heart had started beating but he was now in surgery. From time to time someone would inform me that Tracy was still undergoing surgery, but I had no further information.

Eventually Tracy's cardiothoracic surgeon, Dr. Joseph Flack, came into the waiting room and escorted me to another room where he sat down and, with tears in his eyes, began to tell me that Tracy had died for an hour and a half. Dr. Flack had no idea what happened, why Tracy's heart stopped and why it decided to start again. Due to the fact that Tracy had been without a steady and proper stream of oxygen for such a long period of time he might not wake up. All Dr. Flack knew for sure was that Tracy was now in grave danger and, if he did wake up I should expect that he would remain in a vegetative state.

I was in total shock and followed the doctor's suggestion to go home, as there would not be any answers regarding Tracy's recovery for at least twenty-four to forty-eight hours. And it was suggested that I not be alone.

As I was leaving the hospital my cellphone rang. It was Dr. Flack telling me that Tracy's eyes were moving. This was a critical time and I needed to return immediately to the emergency room where he would meet me and bring me to Tracy in CCU.

It was there that I saw Tracy for the first time after his ordeal. He had all types of tubes coming out of him. There were six computers and monitors on him, he was very bloated and it was obvious that he had gained a lot of fluid weight during the surgical procedures.

I had to look beyond all of that and focus on Tracy. I took his hand, bent down and whispered into his ear, "I love you". And he opened his eyes, squeezed my hand and we began to cry together.

He responded with, "I love you, too."

Tracy:
Strapped down in CCU, I had so much to say, yet could not speak more than those four words I had uttered to Alice. How desperately I wanted to let her know that everything was all right. And to tell her of my journey.

It was several days later that the tubes were removed and I was rejoining the land of the living - in so many different ways.

Physically, my recovery was remarkable; so much so that shortly after the surgery, Dr. Flack walked into the room to visit with me but turned and walked right out assuming I wasn't there. He did not recognize the man lying in bed, head propped up, watching television. It was, indeed, me. I became known as "the miracle man" with all sorts of doctors and medical staff popping into the room just to check me out. And I was finally able to share my extraordinary journey with Alice.

Chapter Eight

Tracy IN HIS OWN WORDS: My Spiritual Journey

While the medical team was frantically working on my physical body, my spirit was on its way to the other side. The first thing that I remember was the total blackness that surrounded me, but I was not afraid. It was like being in bed with the lights out and your eyes closed. I had a sensation of moving at an incredible speed yet not in the physical sense of moving. It was just a sensation. I could see a light in the distance and I became aware of the white path I was traveling upon and it was at that point I realized I was no longer traveling at that incredible speed. Now it was like I had come to a stop, yet I was still moving - as if being given a chance to take in the most stunning and peaceful thing that I have ever experienced. There I was on this white path gazing at the most beautiful bright light in the distance. I instinctively knew I was to travel in the direction of the light. I had conscious thoughts and knew I was dead but I had no fear. There really are no words that would do justice to the beauty and peacefulness of what I was experiencing. As I travelled along this path I began to understand the meaning of certain things but also recognize that once I entered Heaven all of my Earthly questions would be answered. And that was a very comforting feeling.

As I was approaching the light, I felt something stopping me, holding me back. That is when someone (God) spoke to me with a voice that was commanding, yet compassionate and soothing. I was told I could crossover into the light and spend eternity with Him or I could go back and finish the work that hadn't been finished yet. I asked, without speaking aloud, "What have I not finished?" The response was that when the time is right it will be revealed to me. While it was truly tempting to stay and enter Heaven, I thought about Alice and the pain that it would cause her. I also thought about the last thing I had said to her, which was, "Don't worry, Honey. They do this operation all the time. I will be home before you know it." It was at this point I chose to come back to her and the work that I needed to finish (whatever that work was). I knew this was the right thing to do but I also knew that no matter what, there was no wrong choice. It was just my choice to make and make on my own. I didn't understand at the time what that really meant but I do now. I also knew that I would be entering Heaven at some point in the future.

To those who question if I could see my hands or my feet during that time, I respond that I was not aware of my physical body – I was not in my physical body - for I was now a spirit. I was energy with conscious thoughts.

It was clear to me that I had died, but only after having met CJ and hearing her use the term "near-death experience" that I understood it as it related to me.

When I got back and replayed the journey in my mind – over and over again in the weeks and months that followed – I was deeply bothered by the fact that I had not seen Jesus, angels or heard music, and I had not seen any of my loved ones who had passed before. Something was wrong because I knew they were there. Why didn't I see anyone?

Many who have had the same experience say they saw their mothers, fathers, or grandparents when they left this realm. I didn't hear any music; there were no angels and no loved ones. I must say that I felt cheated.

It took the passage of time and much contemplation for me to realize that if I had seen my grandmother with whom I was very close, my decision would have been to keep walking forward into the light and Heaven rather than rejoining Alice back here.

Actually, that realization came to me, as many do, while I was in the shower one morning. That makes perfect sense to me, for what better time to see clearly into your mind and soul then when you are cleansing your body? It was at this point I knew it was all about free will.

What I understood that morning, with the clean water washing over me, was that while on the other side I was given two options, for God, I now know, is all about free will. Yes, we are influenced in our life's choices, often in the subtlest of ways; ways that allow us to make our own decisions. Some of them good. Some not. But they remain our decisions alone. If you make the wrong choice don't worry, God will open another door to make things right once again. Just keep the faith that all will be okay, and it will be in the end.

Being given that freedom of choice, I had often made poor decisions, decisions that ultimately hurt others and, therefore my ego and feelings of worth.

But now I was able to see that while I had always considered myself to be a "bad" person, this was not the case. I was, indeed, a good man who just made poor choices. And now that I was given this second chance at life it was time to make amends and reach out to others with kindness and love.

It's important to remember we are only human and we will make mistakes. God is very quick to forgive us for those mistakes. We, on the other hand, are much harder on ourselves and fellow human beings and aren't so forgiving of those mistakes.

I came back with all of this new understanding of God and choices and His love. This did not come through speech or specific words. It is difficult to explain, but somehow I had been infused with this knowledge. I now know that it does not matter what religion or faith you belong to. We are all worshipping the same God. What the Lord is looking for is for us to have a relationship with Him and to have compassion and love for others. That is how we get to Heaven. There is so much more than just the life here on Earth. Don't get me wrong; life is a beautiful thing that should be cherished. And we should be using our time here to help others, for He is a God of Love.

PART TWO

The Medical and Mind-Body Communities

*"There are no mistakes, no coincidences. All events
are blessings given to us to learn from."
~Elisabeth Kubler-Ross*

Chapter Nine

CJ: Meeting With The Cardiothoracic Surgeons

I had the pleasure and privilege of interviewing Dr. Joseph E. Flack, Tracy's cardiothoracic surgeon at Baystate Medical Center in Springfield, Massachusetts.

We discussed Tracy's experience, covering the event from the medical aspect as well as from the emotional and spiritual perspectives.

Dr. Flack is a diplomate of the American Board of Surgery and the American Board of Thoracic Surgery. He is also a member of the Society of Thoracic Surgery, the Massachusetts Medical Society, the Hampden District Medical Society and a participant on the Heart and Vascular Physicians Task Force at Baystate Medical Center. A man with a great wealth of experience and knowledge to share, he, I knew, would shed much light on Tracy's medical event.

Dr. Flack reiterated the information I had gleaned from Tracy and from the medical team's operative reports: that at approximately midnight of June 5th, 2012, while

Tracy was in CCU recuperating from his bypass surgery, his heart suddenly stopped beating. Resuscitation began immediately, of course, and at 12:15 a.m. Dr. Flack's partner, Dr. Daniel Engelman, the doctor on duty at the hospital, called Dr. Flack. Dr. Flack arrived on the scene about fifteen minutes after that call and joined forces with the team as they tried to bring Tracy's heart back. After unsuccessful defibrillation, the medical team opened Tracy's chest and manually massaged his heart.

During my interview with Dr. Flack, Dr. Engelman came into the room and, so, I was able to speak with him, as well. Dr. Engelman, the son of Dr. Richard Engelman who first brought cardio surgery to Western Massachusetts, holds certifications with the American Board of Surgery and the America Board of Thoracic Surgery and is a fellow of the America Board of Surgery. He is also a member of the Society of Thoracic Surgery, Massachusetts Medical Society and the Hampden District Medical Society.

I questioned both Dr. Flack and Dr. Engelman about why they continued to work on Tracy. Their response was that Tracy was young and they most certainly didn't want to lose him. Yet all the time they were massaging his heart, they felt quite certain there was no way Tracy was going to come back. As a matter of fact, Dr. Engelman told me that during that crucial time he recalls looking over to Dr. Flack on the other side of the operating table and saying, "He's never going to make it." And then he turned to me and continued with, "But we kept going anyway."

It is not unusual anymore, said Dr. Flack, for his medical team to continue resuscitation for an hour or more. What is unusual in Tracy's case, however, is that his blood pressure and oxygen level remained so low. Things were rapidly deteriorating before they were able to get him on the heart-lung machine.

Curious to know if Tracy's recovery has changed the way they evaluate such cases, I asked Dr. Flack and Dr. Engelman if they now treat patients whose hearts have stopped with a different protocol. Both agreed that episodes like this do make them more aggressive in these situations. However, sometimes they do question whether or not to continue. It can be a difficult decision to make. Most often if a medical team brings someone back after a long resuscitation there will probably be neurological damage. But having someone like Tracy gives them hope for future patients. In the emphatic words of Dr. Engelman, "Because of one guy, one guy like this, the rest of your life you try every single thing you can."

When he was able to speak, Tracy had told all around him of his journey to the edge of Heaven and back - his near-death experience. I was, of course, fascinated to know just what Dr. Flack thought about this. He stated that Tracy was not the first patient to share this information.

"And just what do you think about this?" I asked the doctor.

His response was simple and profound, "There is more than we understand."

I need to tell you that hearing this from such an esteemed member of the medical community, a cardiothoracic surgeon who is trained to look for tangible proof to explain life events, thrilled me. It helped validate my growing belief in the truth of the journeys that experiencers (those who have had a near-death experience), have taken. And it gave me a great feeling of comfort and peace.

As I was ending my interview with Dr. Flack, I looked at him and started to ask,

"You are participating in the writing of Tracy's book...."

He finished my question, with, "Why am I doing so? I am helping Tracy on his journey. This has happened. This created a spiritual experience for him and he wants to do something with it and it is partly my responsibility to help him do that. And maybe we'll understand more about these things."

Chapter Ten

CJ: Hearing From Others In The Medical Community

With his thirty-eight years of experience in internal medicine, Dr. Robert Ruxin was the first member of the medical community I turned to for information and clarification. As a layperson I found it quite fascinating – and believed it to be quite extraordinary – that Tracy's heart had stopped for such a long period of time and yet he suffered no significant neurological damage.

Dr. Ruxin agreed with me that yes, this was a rare event, for when the brain is deprived of oxygen for as short a time as four minutes, the cells begin to die and ultimately there is brain death. However, with Cardiopulmonary Resuscitation (CPR) along with other techniques such as were performed on Tracy, oxygen does, indeed make its way to the brain. When I shared with Dr. Ruxin Tracy's medical reports, he stated that it was, in his estimation, very unusual for the medical team to have worked for so long to revive Tracy's heart. And certainly surprising that they were able to supply enough oxygen to his brain to have allowed him to come back with little or no neurological impairment.

Now that Tracy lives in Cape Charles, too far from Baystate Medical Center to continue his medical care there, he has been under the care of a local, highly regarded board certified neurologist in Virginia who has been in practice for over thirty years and specializes in clinical neurophysiology and neurology.

Tracy first visited this doctor on September 30, 2012 with complaints of fatigue, and memory loss. As a specialist in the field of neurology, he gave Tracy a rather comprehensive neurological assessment. His written report of this examination states, in part:

> *"His cognitive impairments are subtle, but definite to this exam … He has a long litany of medical maladies and his near-death experience story is quite intriguing. I am struck by the fact that he has such cognitive reserve and such cognitive ability considering the hour and a half of CPR, which is quite well document[ed]."*

And what about the world of neuroradiology? What might a representative from that discipline, the doctor who specializes in the diagnosis of neurological disease and injury by interpreting medical imaging, think of Tracy's medical event?

In order to find out I contacted Dr. Elliott Mercer who is an interventional and neuroradiologist at Hoag Hospital, Newport Beach, CA.

Dr. Mercer, board certified in Diagnostic Radiology, with a long-established and well-respected practice has over 45 years of experience. And the fact that he, too, was stunned by Tracy's medical case was loud and clear in this, his letter to me:

> *"This is an amazing medical event! If it weren't so well documented I'd have difficulty believing it, but since it is, and everything seems to be "kosher", it's very likely true.*
>
> *As I said previously there had to be CPR and/or other means of supplying blood/oxygen to the brain, kidneys etc. for him to have a chance, and obviously that was the case...*
>
> *I'm not sure that I've seen or heard anything quite this dramatic in my 40 plus years of medical practice----- statistically I'd bet that 99% of people who suffer such an event die, or are in a vegetative state."*

I was in awe that these esteemed men of medicine appeared as amazed as I when reading of Tracy's experience. Reading through various books and articles written by men and women of mainstream medicine, it started to become clear to me that the times are changing as far as understanding the human brain's ability to withstand heart failure, and the necessity to continue working to restart that heart long after tradition would have them do so.

Believing in a near-death experience (NDE) however, is quite a different thing. Most of the medical community is still searching for tangible proof of the existence of an NDE. Unfortunately they won't find it, for there is none to be found.

Some believe that a near-death experience is merely a dream. The experts in the field of near-death experience explain that the major defining difference is that a dream comes and goes; might be remembered but is not life-altering. A near-death experience is most definitely a life-altering event.

And those who would state that the "visions" seen by the experiencer are brought on by the drugs given during surgery and/or resuscitation might do well to heed the words of neuropsychiatrist Dr. Peter Fenwick, world renowned expert on end-of-life phenomena, including near-death experiences and deathbed visions. In his most recent book, "*The Truth in the Light: An Investigation of over 300 Near-death Experiences,*" Dr. Fenwick states,

"The difficulty with those theories is that when you create these wonderful states by taking drugs, you're conscious. In the near-death experience, you are unconscious. One of the things we know about brain function in unconsciousness is that you cannot create images and if you do, you cannot remember them ... But, yet, after one of these experiences (an NDE), you come out with clear, lucid memories ... This is a real puzzle for science. I have not yet seen any good scientific explanation which can explain that fact."

As more people are becoming experiencers; as they feel more comfortable sharing their journeys, the more accepting the general public is in accepting the possibility of the truth of these events. And, accordingly, the traditionalists in medicine are beginning to follow suit.

Chapter Eleven

CJ: Learning Much From A Mind-Body Professional

Like many of us, I have heard of people who have had a near-death experience. But Tracy was the first man I'd met who shared his journey with me and he made such a strong impact that, as I've stated earlier, I felt compelled to share his story with you. In doing so, however, I have the obligation as the author of his book to not just recount Tracy's story, but to learn and explain all that I can about the phenomenon of NDE's.

The term, which was coined in 1975 by Raymond Moody, MD in his book *Life After Life*, has created a field of research that recognizes the near-death experiencer as one who has taken a magnificent journey, and studies the circumstances, contents and after-effects of the NDE.

While information is available on the Internet and in the many books that have been written on the subject, I wanted a more personal and in-depth education and, so, turned to some of the experts in the field.

My good fortune led me to Maggie Callanan, author of *Final Gifts* and co-author of *Final Journeys*. Ms. Callanan is a hospice nurse whose knowledge and reputation are renowned throughout the medical field and that of NDE research.

As we sat and talked over the course of several days, Ms. Callanan shared with me the startling fact that according to the Near-Death Experience Research Foundation, five per-cent of the population has admitted to having a near-death experience. It is quite possible, according to Ms. Callanan and other experts in the field, that the number of experiencers is much higher – many are fearful to share their journeys, for the medical and general population is only just beginning to recognize the veracity of such an experience. She sited a 1992 Gallup Poll that found the number of near-death experiencers in the United States at that time to be thirteen million.

Ms. Callanan was once among the skeptics, for being trained in traditional medicine she thus attributed the experiences to dreams, medication or the oxygen the patient was receiving during the time his or her heart had stopped.

It was when Ms. Callanan began hearing the same information over and over again as she witnessed and heard of NDE's, that she recognized a pattern was forming - one that she could no longer dismiss nor ignore. She started listening rather than merely assuming what the medical community had taught her to believe.

There were distinct patterns in what these patients were saying. And these patterns convinced her that they had, indeed, experienced an NDE.

These patterns are explained by the International Association for Near-Death Studies as the "Four Phases of a Pleasurable Near-Death Experience."

The first occurs when the experiencers feel detached from their bodies, yet are not fearful and are completely at peace. This is the disassociated phase.

The "naturalistic" phase often follows, in which many become aware of their physical surroundings from a spot outside of their bodies.

Next, the "supernatural" phase brings the experiencers to a meeting with beings and environments that are not part of their natural world. This is where they embark on a journey along a white path towards a bright light, might see or hear a higher power, meet with loved ones who have died before them, undergo a life review, and may be invited to enter into the light or return to their physical body. There is complete love surrounding them during this journey.

It is in the final phase, the "return" phase that the near-death experiencer comes back to his or her physical body. Half state that they were given the choice to return and they did so because of a love connection here that they didn't want to leave. The other half said they didn't make the choice but were simply made to return and found themselves back in their bodies.

I asked Ms. Callanan if an NDE is always a religious experience. She said that it is not, and that she knows of atheists who have had NDEs and that their experiences take many different forms. Some don't see a deity or higher power, while others do. However, in many instances the atheist comes back with much to ponder about his or her previous beliefs.

There are similarities in the after-effects experienced by the near-death experiencers and I found them quite fascinating, especially as many are those with which Tracy now lives.

These include a difficulty in being on time. After all, when one has had an extraordinary experience, the ordinary becomes such a bother. This goes for things that require too much structure, such as happened with the IRS agent Ms. Callanan told me about who, after his NDE, had a difficult – nearly impossible – time performing the number crunching his job required. Because the NDE is an infinite experience, being in the finite world of day-to-day life becomes very disconcerting for the experiencer.

The experiencers who were given the choice to come back feel special for being chosen to take this journey. They went for a reason and came back for a reason. And so they are now on an important mission here on Earth – a mission to bring a message of love to all who will listen. Many of those who were compelled to return are angry, frustrated and puzzled, for they were forced to leave a place of infinite peace and beauty and are left with a burning desire to return to it. They have no idea why they had to come back and don't understand what they are supposed to do now that they are here again.

Every one of the experiencers has discovered that his or her life has been changed forever.

Ms. Callanan, convinced that there needed to be support groups for experiencers to share their journeys and recognize that they are not alone, created and coordinated the first National Capitol Chapter of Near-Death Experiencers. There are now such groups throughout the world allowing for near-death experiencers to meet and bring their journeys to the rest of us, so we might begin to understand and accept the reality of these journeys rather than impulsively discounting them.

Yet for all the good work support groups - organizations such as IANDS (the International Association of Near-Death Studies which was founded in 1981 to study and provide information on the near-death experience) - and people like Maggie Callanan are doing to bring the near-death experience to the mainstream of our thinking; to cut through the skepticism that still pervades, there are many who find it impossible to believe. They are looking for proof, some tangible medical proof that near-death experiences are real.

As for those who are still searching for that illusive concrete proof of near-death experiences, well, according to Ms. Callanan, it doesn't exist. But the medical community is finding ways to restart hearts and keep patients breathing longer during times of heart failure and as a consequence we are finding more and more people becoming experiencers. I now accept – along with other non-experiencers – the reality of this extraordinary journey. And have dropped any skepticism I might have once had.

It was rather reassuring to hear about one specific cardiologist who had been sending patients who said they had an NDE to psychiatrists - until he, himself, had a heart attack and became an experiencer. This doctor subsequently took a year off from work during which time he contacted every one of those patients and apologized for having doubted them. He needed to validate them and their experience.

As for those who ask for tangible proof? Well, Ms. Callanan has an answer for that: "Do you love?" she will ask. And when told, that, of course, we love and feel love, Ms. Callanan responds, with a knowing smile, "prove it".

Tracy, the invincible teen

When Tracy met Alice

Tracy at the inn in Cape Charles, VA, September, 2013

Tracy and CJ, September 2013

PART THREE

Karma

"When you live your life with an appreciation
of coincidences and their meanings, you connect
with the underlying field of infinite possibilities."
~Deepak Chopra

Chapter Twelve

CJ: Without A Doubt

When I first met Tracy it was impossible for me to not want further clarification the moment he uttered the line, "And then I died."

Almost delivered as an aside, those four words exploded in the air, filling the room with a volt of energy that shook me to my core. I know what he had said. Tracy had died. Last year. Eleven months prior to my meeting him.

Okay – here was a story I had to explore in more depth. Tracy, being quite open to sharing his journey, was ready and eager to meet with me the next morning in the hotel lobby so I might interview him for what I believed would be a blog or article on my website.

But it grew to be so much more than that.

While Tracy recounted his remarkable story and I typed wildly on my iPad, he told me of the journey that I have now shared with you.

What I learned upon further questioning is that Tracy now possesses a compassion and heightened intuitive awareness of the people around him.

He has an innate sense of to whom he should speak of his near-death experience and when the occasion arises, he does not hesitate to do so.

Shortly after returning to the retirement community where he and Alice worked, Tracy was in the cafeteria when he noticed an elderly gentleman, head bowed in prayer. Going over to him, Tracy gently told him of his recent experience, recounting the beauty and serenity of that place he had recently visited. The man lifted his head and smiled at Tracy, for he had been praying for his wife who was in her room upstairs, dying. Tracy later discovered that this man told his wife that which Tracy had told him, and for the first time in many months, she beamed. She was no longer afraid. She did pass several days later and, some time after the funeral, the man found Tracy to let him know how peaceful she had been at the end, and for that he was so very grateful.

A college-age girl stayed at the inn in Cape Charles not long ago, and in a conversation with Tracy, she told him that she'd recently had a heart transplant. And, so, he shared with her his experience. When she and her parents left the hotel the next day she thanked Tracy and said he had changed her life and she was no longer afraid.

And standing in a grocery checkout line one day, Tracy had a strong urge to share his journey with the woman next to him. It turned out that she, too, had a NDE and was grateful to know he did, as well. She claimed that she'd never met anyone who took this journey. Tracy suspects that she had met many such people. It is just that most don't talk about it for fear of being doubted or ridiculed.

Since his near-death experience, Tracy has been blessed with a heightened vision of the world around him. And he showcases that vision through the stunning photographic skill he now possesses.

He is an avid photographer and his work is striking, finding a new beauty surrounding him that had once been merely a mundane backdrop to his busy life. One of his more recent photos was of traffic on a bridge in a heavy rainstorm. Most would see it as dreary. Through Tracy's lens it is soft and picturesque.

Another detailed a monarch butterfly on a lilac blossom. The timing of taking such a picture was exquisite - the butterfly hanging gently from the edge of the flower.

It was this particular photograph that Tracy gifted to me just before I left him. Upon receiving this present, I sat, quietly contemplating the visual in front of me. Tracy must have thought that I was overwhelmed with the presentation of a gift. Yes, that was part of my reaction. However, and more important, I was, quite bluntly, in shock at Tracy choosing this particular photo to present to me. There was no way he could have known that butterflies and lilacs were my deceased mother's two favorite things. Well, not in any rational way. This was surely another nod from the Universe to let me know Tracy and I were destined to be together that day - much like the unseen force that had originally guided me to the inn in Cape Charles when Alice was not at the front desk so that it would be Tracy who I would meet behind the counter, a mere six weeks after Tracy and Alice arrived there from Springfield.

The picture that most haunted me, however, was one he had taken of two blue glass doors at the entrance to a seaside restaurant. Standing in front of the restaurant Tracy had taken a clear and beautiful shot of the beach behind him reflected in those doors. Everything behind him, in fact, was mirrored in the doors. Yet Tracy himself was not in the reflection - even though he was standing head-on, facing that restaurant entrance. Neither he nor I had an explanation for this phenomenon. We knew that one most certainly existed – perhaps it was the particular camera lens and the setting he had used, or the angle of the sun. Whatever that might have been, it did create great conversation and musing. And made those doors in the photograph all the more intriguing.

The photo that Tracy gave to CJ: "The Monarch"

Tracy's photo of the traffic in the rain:
"Sometimes Life Can Be Blurred"

The photo Tracy took of the reflection in the doors on the beach.
But where is Tracy?

Ultimately, I closed up my iPad, said goodbye to Tracy and Alice, as Joe and I headed off to our next stop: Virginia Beach, Virginia. Upon our arrival, and after checking into a local hotel, we enjoyed a delightful lunch at a Virginia Beach restaurant and proceeded to take a walk along the boardwalk. With the ocean on our left we were thoroughly appreciating our particularly lovely stroll among the other tourists - cyclists, skaters and joggers. But, as it was getting rather windy and cold, we decided to return to our hotel. When we believed we had arrived back at the rear entrance to the hotel, we made a sudden turn away from the ocean to go through its doors. The turn to our right was as abrupt as if an unseen force was pulling me in that direction. But it did not lead us to our hotel entrance at all, for we had inadvertently passed it. Instead of the hotel, I found myself facing the restaurant doors that had been in Tracy's photograph. I suspect everyone within a mile of where I stood could hear my audible gasp.

If there had been any uncertainly that I was meant to meet Tracy and write this book, staring - open-mouthed, wide-eyed, at those doors - obliterated all doubt.

The first thing I did - when I began breathing again - was take the same photo that Tracy had taken and emailed it to him.

Staring at those doors, along with the serendipitous timing of meeting Tracy and having him gift me with the butterfly on the lilac, allowed me to know, with absolute clarity, that our partnership had been sealed.

There was no doubt in my mind that I was meant to be a part of his life and he of mine.

A stylized version of those doors now graces the front cover of this book.

When interviewing Tracy he had stated that he wanted to write a book and when I asked him why, he responded simply and with great caring that his was an experience meant to be shared, to give the message of hope to all who have suffered great loss; that while we mourn, those who have gone beyond are in a very beautiful and peaceful place.

And while we are here on Earth we have the great responsibility to each other to bring kindness into the world in any and every way we can.

And I was meant to write this book because I had come to fully understand the importance of staying open to the messages we are being sent, messages that we often tend to ignore or discredit or scoff at.

When we receive these little pieces of information or find ourselves experiencing a "mere coincidence," I am fully convinced now that there is significance behind each one of these serendipitous events. It is up to us to discover what it is and, when we do, our lives become more enriched as we are guided to continue following our lives' paths with continued meaning and purpose.

I am certain that I am not alone when I ponder the reason behind this life I live; why I am here and what good I can do as just one tiny part of the cosmos. Certainly I have done much good in my life – all I need do is look at my children and grandchildren to recognize that I've had a hand in bringing these beautiful people into the world. But now they are on their own to follow their paths and bring goodness to the world. What lessons can I share with them? With my friends? With those whose paths I intersect as I follow my own journey?

As I am writing this book sharing Tracy's journey, I am realizing the implication of what I am doing that extends far beyond the computer keyboard on which I type. With every person I have spoken to, every bit of information I have read, every word that I have written, I am more and more convinced that I was meant to meet Tracy and share his story. I have become a part of his journey in a meaningful way and it is now my good fortune, and my charge, to share not only my message of keeping one's eyes open for the serendipity of life, but his words to you, the reader.

I shall leave it to Tracy to share with you his message.

Chapter Thirteen

Tracy IN HIS OWN WORDS: An Open Letter To All of Us

Dear Reader,

Now you know that I died for 1 hour and 30 minutes and it is well documented. The following letter to you is part of the reason I have returned. Please read this with an open heart and mind.

I remember lying in the hospital bed in CCU after my near-death experience. That was my home for the next week and a half and time was a bit of a blur. During this time I had a steady stream of doctors and nurses coming to see me. Some of the visits I liked because my visitors wanted to know how I was feeling and wanted to talk to me. Now I know they were trying to figure out why I was talking to them at all, considering the fact I was gone for so long with very little blood going to my brain. Other visits I didn't care for, as they were there to change my sheets or take blood. Now it may not seem like a big deal to change my sheets, but it generated the most intense pain I have ever experienced as I had five broken ribs from the hour and half of CPR. I know they felt bad about it, but the sheet changing served two purposes; one I got clean sheets, but the other was to move me so I didn't get sores from lying in the same position for extended periods of time. The first time a new doctor or nurse would visit my room, he or she would ask me the same question, "What did I remember of my near-death experience?" It wasn't long before I got the nickname, "The Miracle Man." I was feeling pretty damn special, yet at the same time it made me feel uncomfortable because I came back for a reason that has nothing to do with me.

The word was getting out and around the hospital that there was a "Miracle Man" in CCU. Soon I started receiving visits from pastors and priests to question me about my experience. Some seemed to be more accepting to what I had to say, but others seemed to be a bit more skeptical. But that's OK. It really doesn't matter if you believe me or not, just hear the message. I couldn't stop thinking about what God had said to me when He offered me the choice to go back and finish the work that has not been finished yet. What work hasn't been finished yet? And why me? I was nothing special. In the past I was a big time sinner, boozing it up around the world and hurting so many people along the way - not physically, but emotionally. (I'm still a sinner but my sins don't hurt others as in the past, they only hurt me. After all I am only human and at times still make bad choices.) So what did I have to offer others? While I was figuring out what my unfinished work was, I began telling everyone of my journey and told him or her what God is looking for in us.

So, what is He looking for in us? And what is His message for us?

There are three parts to this message:

1) There is a Heaven where we will find eternal peace and beauty.

2) It doesn't matter what religion or faith you follow, because religion is merely a tool to have a relationship with God; which is what He wants more than anything else. Religion also helps you to understand that we each have a unique relationship with Him, for we are all individuals in our own special ways. So we shouldn't impose our relationship on others, but lead by example, so those others can develop their own relationship with God.

3) He is a God of Love and what He is looking for from us is love, compassion, and acts of unselfish kindness to others. We control what we do, as He is a God of free will, but He will try to help us by giving us choices – some choices better than others - but in the end it will be our choice.

The natural question is how do we get to Heaven? The first step is very simple - have a relationship with God.

The second step is to perform a kind act every day for someone. You need to think about doing that kind act, and it must be something that has no personal gain or Earthly reward. Your reward will be waiting for you in Heaven - and what a reward it is. Here's the thing; once you start doing that act of kindness, it becomes a way of life. It really is that simple, for He is a God of Love and Compassion.

This is where some people start having a problem with what I have to say about organized religion. It truly doesn't matter what religion you follow. If you are Catholic, Jewish, Muslim, Christian or Buddhist, at the end of the day you are worshiping the same God. Each faith has it's own name for Him and rules to follow. It is important to understand religion is a tool to help us lead a good life and help us to build a relationship with God. The other thing to remember is that your relationship is yours and yours alone, as mine is mine; it's as unique as you are as a human being. Some people will say I am a heretic or I am speaking rubbish. I have been told I am wrong that if I don't accept Jesus Christ as My savior I won't go to heaven and I am okay with all of it, because it's not about me. I'm just giving the message. My wish is for everyone to try look at it objectively and strip away all the rules of their religion and look at the core essences of religion. What do you have? It's pretty basic; it's for you to have a relationship with God and be kind and compassionate to others.

Now you know what it takes to get to Heaven, but what can you expect when it's time for you to go to Heaven? You will be in the most beautiful place you could ever imagine. You will be greeted by your loved ones who preceded you, and will feel and know the magnitude of God's love for us. For all parents, husband, wives, brothers, sisters and friends that have lost a loved one, the message is that you will be reunited. Those who have gone before us are at total peace and watching over us as we go through our lives. I know the loss of a loved one hurts and it's natural to mourn that loss, but at the same time rejoice in the knowledge that they are in a wonderful, peaceful place where there is no pain, anger, or wars. It is a place of peace and love. And the most important thing of all is that they are with God.

I guess I now know what some of my unfinished work is, and that is to get this message out to as many people as possible. I know there is more to do and it will be revealed when the time is right.

Trust and Believe in Him and love one another, God bless you all.

Tracy LaCroix

Postscript:

Tracy's health at this point is not perfect. He has some heart issues and is dealing with the after-effects of the near-death experience; the same after-effects that most experiencers have, such as memory loss and the inability to concentrate.

He is concerned about Alice, for, as he states, "She has to live with me as I run from task to task, never quite finishing any one when another pulls my attention." His doctors have told Tracy that he must take early retirement and, so, he has to watch Alice go off to work and be their breadwinner. She is quite amazing and Tracy is constantly in awe of her strength, love and support.

Like all - or most of us - he doesn't know what else is in store for him nor what more he will to do in his lifetime, but is open to whatever is waiting for him. Even the eventuality of his passing. And he is not afraid. "Why should I be?" says Tracy. "I've been there on the other side and it is beautiful."

"Each person comes into this world with a specific destiny – he has something to fulfill, some message has to be delivered, some work to be completed. You are not here accidentally – you are here meaningfully. There is a purpose behind you. The whole intends to do something through you."

~Osho

Acknowledgements:

When I first met Tracy and knew that I was going to write this book, I immediately contacted Adria Henderson to request her expert editorial assistance. I knew that she was someone who would not only keep me on my toes grammatically, but would made sure this book recounted Tracy's journey and subsequent message as clearly and accurately as possible. But there was also a hidden agenda in that request, for I knew that she possessed superb interview skills that would be invaluable as we travelled the country meeting with Tracy and the various experts who have helped us detail this amazing medical event. Adria came in quite handy, as well, the day I inadvertently deleted the entire manuscript and contacted her in a panic for help in retrieving it. Of course she did, for even in my most levelheaded moments I cannot hold a candle to her ability to find the most appropriate solutions to any ridiculous problem I throw at her. Adria is still thinking of an appropriate way for me to thank her. While she continues to think, let me simply state my gratitude to her for all she has done to make this book come to life. And for being my "sister."

Many thanks to Tracy LaCroix for opening up his life, his heart and soul to me so we could share his journey and message of hope, peace and kindness with you, our readers. Tracy, just as your near-death experience changed your life, so did meeting you change mine.

And equal thanks to Alice LaCroix for taking such good care of Adria and me when we were in Cape Charles interviewing her and Tracy. She is a woman of infinite poise, good nature and caring.

I thank Dr. Joseph Flack, Dr. Daniel Engelman, Dr. Robert Ruxin and Dr. Elliott Mercer who gave of their time and expertise so the information I put in these pages was true, accurate and up to date. The time these incredibly busy people spent with me – on the phone, via email and in person – is appreciated more than I can possibly express. Thank you for your support, help and contributions to this project.

And to Maggie Callanan, who broadened my knowledge base about near-death experiences, who helped with the title of this book, who assisted me in so many phases and stages of my work, I extend my heartfelt gratitude. It was no mere "coincidence" that you came into my life two years ago. The Universe brought us together for so many reasons – there is much more for you to teach me. I am eager to learn.

I cannot neglect to thank Frank Schipper for deciding that he, Joe and their biking buddy, Rich, should stop in Cape Charles, Virginia. And his wonderful wife, Leslie

Meadowcroft, for choosing that particular hotel for our stay the evening of May 3rd, 2012. Had it not been for those decisions I would not have met Tracy LaCroix and, well, the rest is history.

No acknowledgement is complete without mentioning one's spouse or significant other or best buddy or greatest encourager. So I shall end this list with my husband, Joe, who fits all of the above categories. You are my own personal editor and coach in all of my endeavors, and I am so lucky.

About the Author:

An author and inspirational speaker, CJ Golden has always followed her passion for helping others, while continuing to expand her own horizons in learning to accept the ebbs and flows of life's paths. Through her first two books, workshops and speaking engagements CJ has shared her wisdom with women and girls. Now, having met Tracy LaCroix and learning of his extraordinary journey, she relishes this new opportunity to bring his message of hope, peace and kindness, to all. Tracy's journey was life-altering for him; meeting Tracy was life-altering for CJ. Her desire is that "Reflections From Beyond" will bring the same spiritual serenity to her readers that it has brought to her.

Visit CJ at www.cjgolden.com

Made in the USA
Charleston, SC
16 February 2014